Stephen Cottrell is the Bishop of Chelmsford. He has worked in parishes in London and Chichester, as Canon Pastor of Peterborough Cathedral, as Missioner in the Wakefield diocese and as part of Springboard, the Archbishop of Canterbury's evangelism team. He has written widely about evangelism, spirituality and discipleship. Among his publications are *Walking Backwards to Christmas* (2014), *Christ in the Wilderness* (2012), a series of reflections on the paintings by Stanley Spencer, and books of Lent and Holy Week meditations, *The Things He Carried* (2008), *The Things He Said* (2009) and *The Nail* (2011), all published by SPCK.

The Things He Did

The story of Holy Week

STEPHEN COTTRELL

SPCK

First published in Great Britain in 2016

Society for Promoting Christian Knowledge
36 Causton Street
London SW1P 4ST
www.spck.org.uk

British Library Cataloguing-in-Publication Data
A catalogue record for this book is available from the British Library

ISBN 978–0–281–07623–9
eBook ISBN 978–0–281–07624–6

Typeset by Graphicraft Limited, Hong Kong
First printed in Great Britain by Ashford Colour Press
Subsequently digitally printed in Great Britain

eBook by Graphicraft Limited, Hong Kong

Produced on paper from sustainable forests

For all those who don't know
what to do with themselves

I will recount the gracious deeds of the LORD.

(Isaiah 63.7)

Contents

Contents

Acknowledgements

My thanks go to all those who have supported me in writing this book, especially my mum in whose house in Leigh much of it was written and whose reading through the chapters in their first draft helped me see the book through at least one other pair of eyes; to the team who support me at Bishopscourt – Mary, Jane, Leslie, John and Louise – and help me navigate my way through myriad appointments and challenges and still find time to write; to Rebecca and my family for putting up with the writing on a day off – though this is my hobby! – and to Alison Barr at SPCK for seeing the project through. As with all my books, what I say here arises out of my ministry, my meditating upon and my teaching and preaching about the central mysteries of the Christian faith, so thanks are also due to the people and parishes it is my privilege to serve.

Introduction

This is a book about everything that happens in Holy Week up until the crucifixion. It finishes where many other Holy Week books start.

Many biblical commentators say that the best way of understanding Jesus' ministry is by focusing on what he *did* rather than what he said; and even when he does speak his words are reflections on his actions.

This is particularly true of Holy Week. Jesus stands in the prophetic tradition of those who embody and act out what they teach. He does things. He creates an impact. His entry into Jerusalem on a donkey, for instance, so often thought of as a sign of his humility, is actually a deliberate and politically and religiously provocative act, intentionally acting out the prophecy of Zechariah. Those who knew the Scriptures would have known what was intended.

Overturning the tables of the money lenders can also be read as a means of disrupting the legitimate business of the Temple in order to make the point that the Temple is no longer needed. Washing feet is a sign of a new and different sort of leadership. And so on.

Two of my previous Holy Week books, *The Things He Carried* and *The Things He Said*, focus on Good Friday and

Easter. This book completes the story by looking at these other events in Holy Week that lead up to Good Friday. Each chapter focuses on a different event in the story and brings out the political and religious significance as Jesus moves towards his greatest and final act – his death and resurrection.

These key events of Holy Week – his entry into Jerusalem, his overturning the tables in the Temple, washing his disciples' feet, and particularly breaking bread with them at the Passover – provide the hermeneutical key for what his death and resurrection *mean*. His words at the Last Supper about his body broken and blood shed would have made little sense until after the crucifixion and the resurrection. But then they become the means by which these events are understood and celebrated.

After the Last Supper Jesus prays to the Father that the cup he is being asked to drink might be taken from him, that there might be another way. With the arrest that follows, this event, often referred to as 'the agony in the garden', is a natural conclusion to that stage of his ministry where he is *doing things*. From this point onwards – as he receives the cup – he allows himself to be handed over so that things are *done to him*. This is the meaning of the Passion – both to suffer, but also to become passive, one who is done unto. This is what he carries to the cross – the things we give him, the things we do to him, the things he carries for us, the things God asks of him, and the cup he has to drink. The weight of the cross and all that Jesus carries is explored in the second book, *The Things He Carried*. Forming a trilogy, the story concludes with the things that he says on Easter Day,

The Things He Said. These penetrating words of comfort and enquiry complete the story and point forwards to the new life of resurrection. This book, although written last, completes the trilogy by beginning it.

There is also a link between what is explored in this book and the worship of the Church in Holy Week, particularly the liturgy on Palm Sunday and Maundy Thursday. I hope that those reading the book during Lent will, therefore, be better prepared for Holy Week. If the book is studied in a group there are questions after each chapter to facilitate discussion and reflection.

Most of all I hope the book, like those that preceded it and follow its journey, will take you inside the story of what God has done for us in Christ, the sorrows that he carried for us, the things that he said to us, and here, in this book, the things that he *did*, so that we can see who God is and what our humanity could be.

Finally, I am pleased to be able to include the story of the woman who anoints Jesus at Bethany in the house of Simon the Leper (Matthew 26.6–13). Matthew's account of this story ends with the words, 'Wherever this good news is proclaimed in the whole world, what she has done will be told in remembrance of her.' Unfortunately, the Church's Holy Week lectionaries seem to have overlooked this promise. Far be it from me to suggest that this could be because, generally speaking, lectionaries are compiled by men! But this vital story, telling of what this woman does to Jesus out of her love for him, and in anticipation of his death, and of his acceptance of her (and by association of all who in being served are able to serve others), is missed out. But, surely, this story illustrates the meaning of the things that Jesus did. Having washed his disciples' feet he says to them: 'So if I, your Lord and Teacher, have washed your feet, you also ought to wash one another's feet. For I have set you an example, that you also should do as I have done to you' (John 13.14–15).

Stephen Cottrell

1

---

*He rode into Jerusalem
on a donkey*

J erusalem was in ferment. Knives were being sharpened. Well-worn grooves were smoothed and oiled. Loose tongues wagged. Accusing fingers jabbed. Small children either ran for the cover of their mother's apron or picked up stones ready to join in the excitement. Nobody knew what was happening, but everyone had a theory. They said he was coming: the man, Jesus. They said he was on the road today: the one who restored the sight to that beggar, Bartimaeus (that will put him out of business!); the one who lifted Lazarus from the grave; the one the Pharisees are petrified of. He was coming to Jerusalem, coming to keep the feast. What will he do when he gets here? What will he say?

In a small village near Bethany, close to the Mount of Olives, an unknown man tethered an unridden colt by the first dwelling you would come to if you walked in from the east. Unaware of its place in history, it yawed and brayed, irritated to be tied up and abandoned. And on the road to the east, just small specks on the horizon of a day that had hardly started, a little crowd was gathering and jabbering and coming towards Jerusalem. If you could hear them, then you would hear all sorts of things: laughter, raucous speculation, intrigue, political dissent, religious fervour. All of it was filled with a zealous and uncomfortable intent.

Walking with them, neither at their front nor at their rear, leading them, yet in the midst of them, was Jesus; and while everyone else looked at the road in front of them, or to left and right as if they feared something was about to jump out at them, his gaze was fixed on the distance that was gradually coming towards them, reduced inexorably by every step; his whole life, and the many meanderings of many journeys, converging and fixing itself on this last journey to Jerusalem. He had prepared for it carefully. Mused, not so much on how this day would pan out – how could anyone know that? – but on what it would *mean*. Today was the day when things would be said by the things that he did.

At Bethphage he stopped. It was still early, still a few miles to travel; the fiercest heat of the day was not yet upon them. In the hedgerows corn parsley and rock rose grew in springtide abundance. The fields beyond were speckled red with lilies and poppies. A breeze stirred in the cedar trees behind him. 'Keep on, keep on,' it seemed to say to him, a still small voice fixing his resolve. He turned to two of his followers and whispered to them urgently, the purpose of the day starting to unfold. He said to them, 'Go into the village ahead of you, and immediately you get there you will find a donkey tied up, and a colt with her. Untie them and bring them to me. And if any one says anything to you, just say this, "The Lord has need of them." And he will send them immediately.'

They looked at him blankly, incomprehension masking fear. They knew they were coming to Jerusalem for a reason, but they didn't know what the reason was. Now this strange request. It wasn't what they were expecting, but at least it was something to do. They hurried off into the village and, when they were out of earshot, let their embarrassment turn to gossip and chatter. After all, who was this Jesus? They had seen him do remarkable things; and how could anyone not be impressed when blind men see and evil spirits crouch in fear? These things he did were brilliant, compelling, magnetic. The crowds flocked to him and asked for more. They cheered his every move. They said he was a saviour, a king, someone the Romans would fear, someone who could lead them to freedom.

But now what he said seemed different from what he did. He had started to speak darkly about what might happen to him in Jerusalem. He told a grim story about a vineyard where the workers rebelled against the owner and one by one killed off the messengers and servants that the owner sent to collect his dues, and then killed the owner's son as well, thinking the vineyard could be theirs.

What did this story mean? Did it mean that Israel was a vineyard? That prophets sent by God were killed, and we had killed them? And was Jesus more than a prophet? Not just a messenger, not just a worker of mighty deeds, but a son? And would we kill him as well?

5

Yes, they knew he was from God – no one else could do such things; but a messiah, a king, a son, these were weighty things to carry.

He would only call himself a 'Son of Man', but what did this mean other than one of us? Though those who knew the Scriptures well would whisper that the prophet Daniel had said that 'one like a son of man' would come on the clouds of heaven.

Now, in the days that had led to this day, he had said other uncomfortable things as well. He had taken the Twelve to one side and said to them, 'See, we are going up to Jerusalem, and the Son of Man will be handed over to the chief priests and scribes, and they will condemn him to death.' Or this was what Peter and the others had said he had told them. There was so much speculation in the air. You didn't know what to believe.

Nevertheless, these words had spread like wildfire through the camp. Some just didn't believe it. Others said, 'So why go to Jerusalem?' Others slunk into the shadows, concocting their own plans, either messianic fantasies about Jesus in which he showed people who he really was, blowing them away with some fantastic show of supernatural power, or political revolution, the people rising up and making him king and the Romans forced out the door.

Being asked to fetch a donkey fitted neither picture. Perhaps Jesus was losing it. After all, when James' and John's mother had asked a favour – albeit quite a selfish one – requesting places of honour for her two sons in this kingdom Jesus still spoke about so often, he seemed distracted, irritated, as if his mind were somewhere else entirely. Maybe she didn't know what she was asking for, but what was he going on about when he asked whether they were able to drink the cup that he was going to drink? And come to think of it, what were *they* going on about when, grinning like Cheshire cats, they had said yes? But even that wasn't enough. 'You will indeed drink my cup,' he said, 'but to sit at my right hand and my left, this is not mine to grant, but it is for those for whom it has been prepared by my Father.'

Everything about these words was strange. What was going to happen in Jerusalem? What cups were going to be drunk? What destinies fulfilled? Even his quirky use of the word 'Father' to describe God suddenly jarred with them. How could God be Father? Many people winced at the intimacy and bravado of such a description for God. But Jesus seemed to get away with it, because with him there *was* such an intimacy with God; and if there wasn't, well how did all these things occur?

But now their minds went round in circles. It was getting to the point that whenever Jesus was present they hardly said anything. What was there to say? And when he was out of the room they would argue passionately, putting forward one theory after another, making Jesus what they wanted him to be. But if God is Father, then Jesus is a son. And if Jesus tells me to call God 'Father', then I am a brother and a sister too.

7

They knew this, but they didn't really know where it led. But most of them kept following. The intrigue and expectation in the air led them to believe something was happening; some sort of denouement was upon them. Clarity was around the corner.

So the two of them went into the village. They found it just as Jesus had said.

As they were untying the animals, a few bystanders questioned them. A theft seemed to be taking place under their noses, and they were sure they should do something. But the two of them said what Jesus had told them to say, and the people shrugged and went back to their business. Isn't it always so?

They led the animals back to Jesus, pleased that they had done the job well. He looked at them and smiled. This was something he often did: smiled. It made a difference, especially when the clouds of doubt and confusion engulfed them.

They smiled back. Not saying anything, just throwing their cloaks over the animal for a saddle and handing him the reins.

He took them and turned to everyone else as if to say, it's time to go now. And so the little pilgrimage continued, the day getting hotter, the levels of anticipation rising.

For Jesus, this was a calculated move. None of them understood this. How could they? They didn't understand him. But he reckoned there would be enough people in the crowd who would. It might take a little time. But like a small spark in the dry grass could devour a forest, so it would only take one person to make the connection and the word would spread. Not his word this time, but the words of the Scripture that would come to life and take flesh in him and in the things he did. He would steer a path between the religious and the political fanatics who flanked him and goaded him.

His plan was decisive and humble. It had to be both. The crowds needed – even with help – to come to their own conclusion; and he still needed to be meek. There was no other way for the earth to be inherited. For those who had eyes to see, his actions and their meaning would be plain; and for those who didn't, well, this might open them.

He breathed deeply; the scent of jasmine and wild thyme filled his nostrils, propelled him forwards. He recited the words in his head, the words of a plan and a purpose that had been forming in him for a lifetime: for this is what it meant to be the one who does what no one else could do; to be the one who was God's Messiah, an anointed one, who achieves God's purposes of love by confronting the powers and principalities of death and evil; who becomes the sacrifice that takes sins away. And walking again towards Jerusalem, surrounded again by laughter and intrigue, he didn't know exactly how this would work out in the days that lay ahead of him, and that was hard. Everyone seemed to think he could see into tomorrow. But all he could see was what he had to do. He knew it was of God; that God had called him to this hour. But he didn't know where it would end, except in confrontation and vindication: 'Rejoice greatly, O daughter of Zion! Shout aloud, O daughter Jerusalem! Lo, your king comes to you; triumphant and . . . riding on a donkey.'

These were the words that had seized him, and over the years, as he had searched the depths of his vocation, it had come down to this journey and all that would be announced in the manner of his impending arrival.

And so he rode the colt towards Jerusalem. As he rode along, other people came out, and some of them began to spread their cloaks on the road. They chattered to one another about what this entry into Jerusalem might mean, and the gossip spread through the crowd. This is what the prophet foretold. This is how the king arrives.

And others built upon it. Like all good stories it spread and grew with the telling. He may look meek and gentle. But kings come to sit upon thrones and to establish kingdoms. That is what he is coming to do.

From the path into Jerusalem down by the Mount of Olives the crowds were getting larger and stronger, more confident and more vocal. Some went ahead of him singing and shouting. Others followed him. Right at the front, a young man turned cartwheels and another walked on his hands. Tearing down branches from the trees, the crowds laid these in his path, along with their cloaks. Children waved palms. Everyone sang lustily and praised God joyfully, shouting out the deeds of power they had seen, and whipping each other into

10

a frenzy so that they would expect more. 'Blessed is the king who comes in the name of the Lord!' they shouted. 'Peace in heaven, and glory in the highest heaven.' And then, 'Hosanna to the Son of David. Hosanna in the highest heaven!'

These hosannas echoed through the air. It was like a little army was entering into a city to make it their own. Or was it just a carnival, a happy, boisterous parade, and tomorrow the town would be back to normal?

There were Pharisees in the crowd. They observed the procession towards Jerusalem with a grim and restless discontent. This Jesus was trouble. They had known it for a long time. Now they could ignore it no longer. They had tried to contain him, like you might shut the door on a hornet, keeping it in one room and preventing its invasion of the house. But this strategy was no longer working. What had they expected? That he would fly around in circles and drop exhausted from the sky? Or sting himself to death? Something had to be done, for now – or so it seemed – others were forcing open the door and a whole swarm of locusts was about to descend.

They folded their arms and drew their cloaks tightly around themselves. They would not be contaminated. They would not be invaded. They would not have their power questioned or their authority undermined. Their carefully constructed detente with Rome, which was, after all, for the sake of this people who now seemed set on making someone else king, would not be disrupted so easily.

How fickle is the human heart. How lonely is the exercise of power. They felt the burden of the moment and its heat, and in that moment resolved to act – though how and when they didn't yet know. Standing in Jesus' path they said to him, 'Teacher' – for they still had this much fear of him – 'order your disciples to stop.' But he answered, smiling defiantly: 'I tell you, if these were silent, the stones would shout out!'

When they came to that bend in the road where the holy city in all its marvellous beauty is laid out before you in the shimmering sunlight of a bright day, he stopped. He stopped as if some invisible force were pinning him to the spot. He dismounted and looked around him as if suddenly confused by his surroundings and the rising tide of the acclaim. He stopped, and his whole body convulsed with a violent and terrible sorrow. Weeping, he cried out: 'O Jerusalem. Jerusalem, if you, even you, had only recognized on this day the things that make for peace! But now they are hidden from your eyes. Indeed, the days will come upon you, when your enemies will set up ramparts around you and surround you, and hem you in on every side. They will crush you to the ground, you and your children within you, and they will not leave within you one stone upon another; because you did not recognize the time of your visitation from God.'

The tears ran down his face. Nothing could stop them. At first he was just mumbling, repeating the same words over and over. But then he raised his voice and said it again, how

Jerusalem itself and all it stood for had somehow failed and would be cast down.

Those who were closest to him, who heard him say to the Pharisees how the stones would sing out God's praises if the people stopped, and then how these same stones would be broken and crushed because they did not recognize God when he came, were confused and fearful. A shadow passed across the brightness of the day. Compared to his anguish and this inundation of his tears, the thunderous acclamation of the people that still echoed in the air seemed but a whisper.

Crowds that quickly gather, just as quickly disperse. He had known it before. It was already starting to happen again. People looked at each other and shrugged their shoulders. 'What now?' they seemed to be saying. And the weeping man, like the earth, required nothing.

The colt that had been brought unwillingly into the centre of the day's drama brayed furiously. It broke the tension in the air. Some people started laughing. A small child cried and ran to find its mother. Others too looked around for the security that he had appeared to offer but had now, with these tears and these words, suddenly withdrawn. They wanted him to be their leader, and surely that was what this day meant, coming into Jerusalem on a donkey just as the prophet had foretold. That was what had scared the Pharisees; that much was sure. But there wasn't much else to hang on to. He didn't look like a leader now. He walked towards Jerusalem as if in a dream, and the salt of his tears lay unwashed upon his face, plain for all to see.

For reflection

- What did you make of this chapter?
- What feelings did it evoke in you? What experiences did it remind you of?
- What questions does it raise for you?

Read Luke 19.28–44.

- What strikes you most about this passage?
- Why were the people so excited?
- Why did Jesus weep when he saw Jerusalem?
- What do you think Jesus is doing in this story?
- What was its meaning then, and what might be its meaning for us today?

2

---

*He overturned the
money changers' tables*

Like a circle of amber in the fist of the sky, the noonday sun burned defiantly. Almond and acacia trees were in bloom. The air was heavy with the sharp perfume of their scent. That, and the expectation in the crowd, whose fists were also clenched.

They followed him. With all sorts of motives and for all sorts of reasons. Some were anxious or battling pent-up anger. Others were excited, bewildered or bewitched. The kettle was boiling. Hissing insistently. But no one could lift it from the heat. There was an incessant whistling in the air people simply couldn't ignore.

His tears had passed. His vision was clear. Through the winding streets of Jerusalem he went, striding out, purposeful, determined. Nobody spoke to him. The joy of his entrance had been overtaken by the foreboding over what he was going to do next. Everybody sensed where he was going. But nobody said anything or knew why. They followed in the slipstream of his resolve.

When the outer walls of the Temple came into view, he stopped. And abruptly. It was as though an invisible wall had halted his progress and held him in check.

The Temple. God's house. The place on earth where the mysterious beauty of God's presence dwelt. This was the place where sacrifice for sin was offered. This was the place where the people offered their sacrifices day after day; and where the priests came doing their priestly things year after year. This was the place where the High Priest came once a year, and entering behind the second curtain went into the Most Holy Place, to the golden altar of incense and the gold covered ark of the covenant containing the golden jar of manna and Aaron's blooming staff and the stone tablets of the covenant itself. And always coming with blood: the blood of the sacrificed Passover lambs; the blood of bulls and goats; the blood to signify deliverance and atonement. This was what the Temple was for. Tremendous and majestic, it loomed before him. Its beauty and its purpose cast a spell over the people. It drew them in. It towered above him, stretching to left and right, its walls absorbing and echoing the praise of a nation hungry for God and crying out for freedom, a people charged with a terrible destiny to be the light of all the nations and the way to peace with God.

Oh, how this nation had ebbed and flowed, sometimes victorious, sometimes faithful, but many times treacherous and fickle and going its own way. Other gods and other sacrifices and other altars had often seemed more alluring. The God who had revealed his name as the present tense of being, the one who acted *in* history and not just above it, had sometimes been too hard to follow and the spectacular variety of the gods of more powerful nations had seemed preferable. But as they abandoned God, so they had also returned; and so this faithful God had raised up men and women of purpose and faith to reset the compass of their faith. Their historic vocation remained intact despite exile and defeat. And now, the Temple, rebuilt and restored, more glorious than ever, and spanning acres, spoke to all who passed by of God's dominion. Yet at the same time it was held in the firm and unyielding grip of Roman control; God and God's people tied down, tolerated and subdued. That is why both people and scribes searched their Scriptures for a saviour, and were ready to back Jesus when he came – or cut him loose if he let them down.

Perhaps that was why he stopped: the enormity of it all, or his own doubts, fixing him to the spot? Or was it God's much trumpeted but rarely seen compassion presenting him with a choice?

The crowd behind him muttered under their breath. Everyone had their own theory. Nobody was very sure. Conjecture and assumption filled the air. What was going to happen now? What was he going to do?

He took a deep breath, holding the air in his lungs as if it were a last breath. He looked around him, his eyes beckoning his followers to come close. None of these so-called chosen twelve disciples looked very courageous then. They shuffled forward. He wanted them with him, but he offered no instructions.

Then he moved. Striding forward towards the Temple. Through the gates and into the outer court of the Gentiles, the place where money is changed and animals for sacrifice are bought and sold. It was its usual hot bustle of people and noise. What had once been a quiet place where all the peoples of the world could come and pray (the inner court was, of course, reserved for the Jews) had now become a marketplace for the necessary business of getting the right money for the right animal for the right sacrifice that would make peace with God. Beyond it, invading the nostrils and cancelling out the perfume of the spring flowers, was the stench of death. Behind the walls and in the Temple itself, pigeons and goats were being killed. This is what sacrifice entails. Throats being cut. Blood being spilled. Entrails dropping. Flesh burning. The whole macabre round of covering your sin and making your peace, day after day, year after year, death after death after death.

Suddenly there was violence and foreboding in the air, and it emanated from him. He was a tornado, a whipping frenzy of righteous rage in the midst of all this commerce and clamour. He was turning over the tables of the money changers, lifting them with both hands, and sending them crashing to the ground, pushing them this way and that. He was upending the benches where those who sold doves were going about their lawful business. His stamping feet were beating out a rhythm of change and putting his mark upon the place.

Gold and silver coins tumbled to the floor and sparkled in the dust. Greedy hands stretched out to grasp them. Doves and pigeons shackled on death row received a last-minute amnesty as their cages crashed to the ground. A few stretched their wings and soared into the sky. Surprised by liberation, and ill equipped for freedom, their wings diminished and forlorn, others pecked among the dust. Wasn't it ever thus? Why is darkness so attractive? Why are prison walls so safe?

It happened so quickly that half a dozen tables were thrown over before anyone even tried to stop him. It just happened. Everyone was too surprised and too bewildered even to move, let alone prevent him. He passed through them like the angel of death itself, deftly extinguishing light after light, and for a moment no one could lay a hand on him.

But now people saw him. It was Jesus. The Nazarene. *Mad after all.*

People screamed and laughed. Some ran for cover. One vomited in fear.

Others had him in their sights. Some of the money changers whose tables were further into the court hurriedly gathered up their profits in their arms and stuffed their money into leather purses and ran. Others were ready for a fight. They stared with icy opprobrium at his advance.

And now people were trying to stop him. Hands reached out to detain him, to catch hold of him. People stepped in his way. But it was still happening too quickly. It was too confused.

Jesus was at the centre of a maelstrom.

Tables were upended. Fights were breaking out. But most people were more concerned with saving their money or grabbing a piece of the action than actually stopping him.

Around him his disciples looked dumbfounded and inept: incapable of joining him, they were equally incapable of stopping him. Those who recognized them as followers of Jesus screamed at them out of their own frustration and displeasure.

Children cried and turned to find their mothers. Mothers cried and turned to find their children. Old men closed their eyes.

He swept through the courtyard like a man possessed of God, as if the Temple itself was suddenly being made redundant.

And then he stopped.

He turned, defiant and breathless at those who pursued him. His eyes blazed. It was a look that would turn you to stone; and even those who wanted nothing more than to lift him up and turn him over and give him the flavour of his own medicine, also stopped. An uneasy stillness, as if this could escalate further if they didn't stop for a moment, and an ominous silence fell upon everyone. Not the silence of peace: more the silence of a coiled spring about to jump; or a bowstring stretched to its extremity and about to be released with a brutal finality; or the silence of a waiting battalion lined up for battle, the general about to give the order to advance.

Everyone breathed deeply. No one dared look at anyone else. All eyes were fixed on him. Was this the time to devour him? Was this where it will end?

He lifted up his hands. Not in surrender, but to heaven, as if some great proclamation was about to be made. He cried out: 'My house shall be called a house of prayer; but you are making it a den of robbers.'

Then another silence fell. Part shame and part remorse, it prevented people from moving or acting. The violence that had been in the air dispersed. People brushed themselves down. They picked up their tables. They gathered up their coins and sorted them into neat piles. They shrugged their shoulders and smiled. Conversations started again. The doves that had not yet flown were gathered back into their cages. Normal business will soon be resumed.

But what had Jesus meant: a den of robbers? 'We are not doing anything wrong,' they said to each other.

And they were right. Yes, they were making a profit from these prayers, but what is profit other than another word for a living? In the main these were not rich or dishonest men. They were doing what had to be done. They were doing what the law required. 'He wants to destroy the

Temple itself,' says one. 'That is the meaning of this action. He doesn't just want to put us out of business. He wants the whole thing stopped!'

And for a little while that day, that is what happened, that is what Jesus did. He stopped the Temple in its tracks. Its unending round of exchange and death stopped for a little while. It stopped because the one who was himself a temple, a place where God's glory dwelt on earth, came; and not yet offering a final sacrifice, prevented the means of production for all those little sacrifices that in their way foreshadowed his.

He knew what he was doing. Growing inside him was the painful knowledge of what he had to do. He didn't like it, and he didn't quite know how and when, but shadows of what was to come kept crossing his path, and for him this was another sign that pointed the way to meaning and conclusion. Of course it had to be in Jerusalem. Of course it had to be Passover. Of course it had to be *now*, for this was the hour that God had led him to. He couldn't see it as you might imagine. He couldn't see the future in the same way that we see the past. For him it was like looking on a vine in springtime. It yields so many shoots, and each one is capable of bearing much fruit, but unless pruned will become overburdened by its own abundance and the fruit will fail, never reaching its potential. So it is pruned and pruned, till only one stem remains. So there is no doubt. This is the one that will bear the fruit, and that fruit will come when the time is right.

Hardly anyone else got it. Not even his closest followers. They still thought he would jump from the trap that was being laid. That is why they had asked for places at his left and right in glory. They could only see victory, and they wanted recognition and honour when the prizes were being handed out. They only saw the harvest, never the tilling of the soil, or the painful pruning of the plant. They just didn't understand the things he was doing and where they would lead. No one did. Nor did they understand the type of victory he would win and the dreadful manner with which this victory would be achieved. So very quickly, even this astonishing act of cleansing was seen as a judgement on the ethics of their business practice, and not on the Temple itself.

'They must have been short-changing the people,' one suggested; and everyone agreed that this was what his actions meant. They even joked about it, or at least joined in the jokes that were quickly doing the rounds across Jerusalem as the day drew on. After all, hadn't he spoken about destroying the Temple before? He had even said he could raise it up again in three days. That was a laugh. It had taken generations to build.

But these actions still had about them a brutal purpose that shocked everyone, especially those closest to him. Their jokes hid their unease. They were mainly just glad it was over and the tension was lifted from the air.

They watched him withdraw into the crowd. Some of them even dared to hope it might be over. None of them could see what was beginning.

As he disappeared from their sight, they saw another crowd gathering around him. It was a familiar one, the one he gathered everywhere he went: the blind and the lame, small children and widows. They flocked to him.

His friends couldn't see him any more. They could just see all the people that needed him thronging around him. They were reaching out to touch him and he didn't stop them. The music that was in him chimed with the music in them. Dispensation flowed from him, and like that spring of water that the prophets say might flow from the Temple itself, it ran like healing streams into their hearts and lives.

He changed people. That was the fearsome beauty of the things he did. His presence, his touch, his actions, his words, they did things to people's lives. Therefore why put it all in jeopardy? Why antagonize and confront? Why come to Jerusalem at all? For in another part of the courtyard, the chief priests and teachers of the law were themselves taking council together. They had seen what he had done, and they had reached their conclusions. The man was trouble. He endangered the delicate harmony of the *entente cordiale* they had established with Rome. He disturbed the people. He gave succour to fanatics. He threatened their power. He raised false hopes. He was therefore a false prophet. He had to be removed. It was as simple as that.

For reflection

- What did you make of this chapter?
- What feelings did it evoke in you? What experiences did it remind you of?
- What questions does it raise for you?

Read Matthew 21.12–17.

- What strikes you most about this passage?
- Why do you think Jesus overturned the tables of the money changers?
- Why are the chief priests and scribes so angry with Jesus? What is it about him that so infuriates them?
- What do you think Jesus is doing in this story?
- What was its meaning then, and what might be its meaning for us today?

3

*He ate with
tax collectors and sinners*

In the end this was his undoing. He just wasn't respectable enough. He mixed with the wrong sort of people. He wasn't one of us. There was too much God in him, and not the 'God-fearing sort of God' the God professionals liked to peddle. His was a very down-to-earth God: a compassionate 'on your side' God; a completely understanding and 'why not start again' God. And it drove them mad, the God professionals, the scribes and Pharisees, the ones whose job it was to tell people who God was and who God wasn't, and what following God looked like. They had the certificates to prove it. And the breeding. And he didn't. After all, they sneered at him – 'Has anything good ever come out of Nazareth?'

When people started stoning a woman caught in the very act of adultery, he sat and drew in the sand and invited the one who had never sinned to cast the first stone. When the wine ran out at a wedding he called for six stone jars of water and they amazingly turned into wine. And not just any old cheap plonk, but the finest vintage. When the crowds were hungry he fed them – all of them – with one boy's lunch. He did amazing things. The crowds loved it and

31

followed him wherever he went. Blind people received their sight. Lepers were cleansed. Small children blessed. When he arrived late at the tomb of his dear friend Lazarus he wept, but he also cried out to God and called Lazarus from the grave, and, removing the cloths from his 'just that moment ago cold corpse', Lazarus came forth. Nobody understood it. Nobody could control it. Even he seemed to play it down, telling a cripple who had just started walking not to tell anyone what had happened. Well, how does that work? How do you keep that a secret?

He called these actions 'signs', not miracles. If he spoke about them at all it was in riddles. Or stories. He made you laugh, that's for sure. He was a good storyteller. He could talk the birds out of the trees. But the things he did, oh they were wonderful, and they were mysterious. They were signs pointing to something else, pointing to abundance and a healing that was in him, but not in a way even he could obviously or easily control. He wasn't turning on a tap, or flicking a switch. He was a channel. And his faithfulness and obedience to be that channel meant streams of living water were always flowing.

He called God 'his father'; and it was this Father God that did these things in him and pointed him towards the same abundance that we saw in him, in all those signs, and in all those wonders.

And he ate with all the wrong sort of people. He kept very bad company. He got in with a rum lot. And he didn't care what people said or thought. He wasn't trying to please them, only God.

In that week, as one thing led to the next, he would withdraw to Bethany to his friends; and one day, eating in the home of Simon the Leper, his disciples with him and others laughing and jesting, a woman came in from the street carrying an alabaster jar of costly ointment, pure nard. She didn't say anything. She didn't have to. She had about her an air of quiet determination and a devotion that had already passed beyond the cares of what others may say. She knelt at Jesus' feet. She broke the seal on the jar, and gently, lovingly, poured the oil on to his head.

Everyone stared in disbelief. Was he really going to let this woman do this to him? Wouldn't he stop her?

But that is one of the amazing things about him. He lets other people do things to him. He doesn't prevent them. In fact, he rebukes those who get in the way, who think they are protecting his dignity by erecting all sorts of barriers and qualifications around him. 'Let the little children come to me; do not stop them,' he once said to his disciples who assumed that he would be far too busy to worry about children.

Oh, but he wanted people to come to him. What he did, and what he goes on doing, is opening his arms wide. He stretches them out in welcome to the world. So this woman, whoever she was and whatever she had done, and in spite of the prohibitions of his religion saying women, and for that matter lepers and small children, are not people to mix with, that they are unclean, he goes to them and he lets them come to him. He enjoys their company. He sees in them the very humanity he has taken to himself. He loves them.

So she pours the oil upon his head. It is warm, and its fragrance fills the air, musky and sweet. It gently trickles down his neck and on to his beard. He smiles at her, full of simple gratitude for the gift of this anointing. There is a joy between them.

But the others around the table – his disciples and all the rest – are agitated and angry. This is expensive ointment. And this is a woman of possible ill repute, and anyway, a woman. What right does she have to do this? And where did this oil come from? It must have cost a fortune. Did she steal it? And if there is money to throw around on oil, wouldn't it be better to give it to the poor? Yes, that is the line they take. A sudden concern for others bolsters their effrontery. After all, the best way to protect your own bank balance is to offer the very best advice to others about what they should do with theirs. It is as if talking about giving is itself enough.

But what she does is just give; and she goes on giving. And what he does is receive, and he goes on receiving. It is almost as if Jesus is not listening to the puffed-up yammer of their indignation. He has screened out the good advice and the implied good intentions of the extravagantly self-righteous who actually intend to do nothing, and is, instead, focused on the one who gives and is able to receive. He is undefended. And it is the shocking beauty of this generous vulnerability that draws all those who also long to receive and are able to offer themselves.

This is what he loved about the poor. They were so generous. He called it 'poor in spirit', which was more (or is it less?) than the actual amount you possess, but an attitude to what you have, a sense that everything is gift, and that it comes unearned and undeserved. We enter this life with nothing. We leave with nothing, and in between it is a proper poverty of spirit that enables us to live with joyful gratitude and generosity, thankful for whatever we have and for the good God who gave it to us (as he gives everything) and, therefore, how could we not share it and go on sharing?

Even yesterday he had sat again in the Temple square opposite the Treasury as the days of this holy week numbered themselves towards the feast of Passover itself, and had watched as an elderly woman, a poor widow, made her offering. Many rich people put in large sums (large sums they could afford, that is, and in so doing looked forward to a favourable mention in dispatches and their names engraved on plaques or pews) and she put in two small copper coins. While they had given from their abundance, she, by giving from her poverty, had put in everything she had.

Now this woman with the oil. The only thing those around him could think of was its cost; not the cost to this woman who had purchased the oil and sought him out and braved their reproach and done this thing of kindness, but the money itself.

They were still rehearsing the lines of their indignation, each one more piqued than the other, when their voices reached him. All voices do eventually. So he turned to them and said, 'Why do you trouble the woman? She has performed a good service for me. For you always have the poor with you, but you will not always have me. By pouring this ointment on my body she has prepared me for burial. Truly I tell you, wherever this good news is proclaimed in the whole world, what she has done will be told in remembrance of her.'

Another shadow crosses the day. They stare at him, dumbfounded. He is very irritating. Not only does he accept this woman's offering. Not only does he shame them in front of her, reminding them that there will always be poor people to serve (and is he suggesting they should do it? Doesn't he know that they would love to serve the poor if they could, it's just that their resources are so limited?), now he says that he won't always be around. He says that this anointing is for his burial.

Everyone looks aghast. It is good to sit and eat with him. But it is also so hard and uncomfortable. He is one of those people that as soon as you think you've got him worked out goes and does something to confound you.

They sit around his table and they are covered in embarrassment. They don't really know why. Nothing is as they expect it to be. Have they come to Jerusalem for life and for victory, or for death and defeat? Will they even know what each one looks like? They know the religious authorities have it in for him. But there isn't really any evidence. Apart from this. Their constant gripe: he eats with tax collectors and sinners. He doesn't deny it. He revels in it. He seeks out the lost. He embraces those who must not be embraced. He makes himself unclean and then calls them – the scribes and Pharisees, the keepers of the law – dirty. That was their complaint. And he gave as good as he got. He called them blind guides who strained a gnat but swallowed a camel; whitewashed tombs that looked lovely on the outside but inside were full of bones. He called them hypocrites who did not go into God's kingdom themselves but stopped everyone else. And when they complained about him and the company he kept, he just smiled and said, 'Those who are well have no need of a doctor, only those who are sick.'

Sitting round the table, his head dripping with the oil of an anointing which was for death, they too felt ashamed, were painfully aware of the muddled compromises of their own hypocrisy, even though they were his friends and his guests, and they ached for the medicine that only he could bring. To look at him and the things he did was a healing; it was like looking in a mirror and seeing what humanity was supposed to be like and seeing yourself as you could be. Such a vision of a changed and redeemed humanity was

37

wonderfully compelling. But it was also deeply challenging. He knew that some would embrace him and, weeping with lament, ask to be healed and set free. But others would harden their hearts and turn away. This was the one thing he couldn't do: make people's choices for them. Everyone had to make their own. They sat around the table in silence pondering which way to turn. The dice span in the air.

One of the Twelve who was there around the table was particularly indignant. He had put a lot of trust in Jesus. He had followed him since the beginning. He had seen Jesus do wonderful things. He had thrilled at his rhetoric. He had longed for his kingdom. He had believed in him. But this belief was starting to waver. Jesus was looking less like a king and more like a servant. He didn't like this. It wasn't right. He didn't really know who Jesus was any more; or even what he wanted him to be; or whether this would only become apparent if the pace of events was pushed a little. His motives were desperately confused. He was angry, but he didn't really know why.

Later that day he went to the chief priests. He thought there was probably enough evidence against Jesus for them at least to arrest him. He said that he could tell them where he was. They were very pleased and offered him money in return for his service.

From that moment, Judas looked for an opportunity to betray Jesus.

For reflection

- What did you make of this chapter?
- What feelings did it evoke in you? What experiences did it remind you of?
- What questions does it raise for you?

Read Matthew 26.6–16.

- What strikes you most about this passage?
- Why were the people so outraged by this woman's actions?
- Why is Jesus so accepting?
- Why do you think Judas betrays Jesus?
- What do you think Jesus is doing in this story?
- What was its meaning then, and what might be its meaning for us today?

4

He washed his disciples' feet

Thursday evening was Passover day, the Jewish festival where they remembered their liberation from slavery. Jesus had planned it carefully. An upper room in a discreet part of the city was booked and a Passover meal prepared. Threads were being gathered together. The tapestry would soon be complete. For those who had eyes to see, the knotted skein at the back of the loom was all that was visible at the moment, and it made no sense. But the loom would be turned around. It would reveal something beautiful.

When he arrived with his disciples it was as if Jesus knew that this night and this Passover was one of special significance. It would provide the lens through which everything that followed would be seen and understood, just as the Passover itself was the blueprint for the supper where he himself would be food and drink.

Having loved his own who were in the world, he loved them to the end.

In the rest of the city similar preparations were being made. There was a buzz and an excitement in the air. Festivals are always exhilarating. People were rushing home, dressing up; all over the city tables were being laid.

The heat of the day was subsiding. A cool breeze was blowing in from the east. The sky was scorched and marbled with streaks of violet and pale vermillion. Above the city, two eagles rode the evening thermals, circling and looking for prey.

During the meal Jesus got up from the table. He took off his outer robes. He tied a large towel around his waist. He poured water into a basin and started to wash his disciples' feet and wipe them with the towel. He did it so unobtrusively that at first they hardly even noticed it, thinking perhaps that someone else had entered the room and a servant was doing this for them.

But when they saw it was Jesus, that he was their servant, they looked at him with a kind of dumb disbelief. Why was he, their master, demeaning himself in this way? But he worked quietly, methodically and thoroughly. He smiled throughout. And they just sat there and let it happen. He was, in those moments, a still small voice in their presence; a voice of service that did this simple act of love with simple deliberation.

It shut them up. For a moment. They received from him, and this was never something they were very good at. Like most people, they were always happier to be in control, defining themselves by their power over others. But what he did was so obviously 'other' that it silenced them. The whole order of their expectations was upended, and they felt embarrassed, feeling they would never get to the bottom of him. After all, hadn't he reproached them when they argued among themselves about who was the greatest? He had said the first must be slave of all, and that the Son of Man – whom they assumed to be a reference to himself – came not to be served but to serve, and to give his life as ransom for many. But surely he meant servant of God? Not *their* servant? Yet, here he was, washing their feet. The things he did were too hard to fathom. The things he said were conundrums. He challenged everything.

It is a funny thing having your feet washed. Feet are more private than hands; on display each day, but rarely looked at or loved. They are not objects of beauty. They are gnarled and sweaty. They bear the brunt and weight of the day. Their skin is broken and rough. They are not accustomed to attention. If they are washed, it is usually a perfunctory thing. But he held their feet tenderly. He knelt before each one of his disciples and, holding their feet firmly and before he washed them, he looked each one of them in the eye. He held them with his gaze, and his eyes sparkled with gladness and affection. His eyes said, 'I know you; and I want to do this thing for you because I love you; and I want you to be clean. And I will wash away the heat and burden of the day. I will be with you as one who serves. Come to me all who are weary and overburdened, and I will give you rest. I will make you clean. I will make you well.'

And what can you say to that? Even if you are feeling a little stupid, or slightly vulnerable, or just embarrassed, it was good to feel the cool unction of the water and his steady grip, holding and kneading your feet.

So that is what he did. He moved from one person to the next. He washed everyone's feet. But when he got to Peter it was different. Everyone was feeling a mixture of awkwardness and delight as he did this thing, but only Peter objected. When Jesus held Peter's feet and looked him in the eye, Peter tried to pull away. 'Lord, are you going to wash my feet?' he asked with stubborn incredulity.

This wasn't really a surprise. Peter had always been difficult. He had a knack for getting things wrong. If the stick had a wrong end, he would unerringly go for it and pick it up. He was the natural leader – likeable, affable, capable in a 'doing things' sort of way – but also headstrong and boastful, easy to forgive and, therefore, often in need of forgiving. When he had first encountered Jesus he had said to him, 'Go away from me, Lord, for I am a sinful man!' This turned out to be an isolated incidence of self-knowledge. After that he promised everything, but delivered little. Even his name – Peter – was something of a joke. It meant 'rock'. It was the name Jesus had given him, but it was not a name he lived up to. 'Sandy' would have been more appropriate, for that was what he was like. He looked good. He sounded good. But like a house built without foundation, come the crisis he would always collapse.

He had been the first to glimpse who Jesus might be. When others called him 'rabbi' or 'prophet', he had boldly declared, 'You are the Messiah.' All the other disciples had grinned in vacant disbelief at this. But Jesus took it. He took it not just because Peter had said it, and he so obviously loved Peter, but because he always saw something in him that others couldn't. Somewhere inside Peter's bravado was an ability to grasp things and reach beyond himself to become that person that Jesus could see. But when Jesus then started talking about being rejected and killed, Peter got it wrong again. He wanted it his way. He wanted Jesus as his sort of Lord, not one that would suffer, not one that would die. So Peter rebuked Jesus, saying it could not and need not end like this. And Jesus said to him, 'Get behind me, Satan.'

You see, Peter was one of those people who got things right and got things wrong at the same time. When he made his promises he really meant them. But he couldn't see them through. He was still too full of himself, to let anyone else in. Too busy talking, to ever really listen. Too scared of dying, to ever really live.

Then there was that stormy night on the lake. Jesus had just fed thousands of people, and everyone was exhausted and elated. He dismissed the crowds and sent the disciples in the boat to the far shore. A terrible storm blew up from nowhere, like it sometimes does in these parts. The wind was against them and the waves were enormous, battering the boat and crashing over them. They thought they were going to die. Then, in utter amazement, they saw Jesus walking towards them upon the water and out of the eye of the storm. At first they thought it was a ghost. They cried out in fear, but Jesus said, 'Take heart, it is I; do not be afraid.'

Peter answered, 'Lord, if it is you, command me to come to you on the water.'

Jesus said, 'Come.'

So Peter – dear, deluded, brave and foolish Peter – got out of the boat and started walking on the water towards Jesus. At first it worked. It seemed that when he was held by Jesus' gaze he was safe, he was able to do the things that Jesus did. But the winds were still strong, and Peter was still Peter; still more full of himself than ready to be filled by God. So he looked around him. He saw the forces raged against him. He thought they were stronger. After all, isn't that the sensible thing to think? Isn't that what we all think? Filled with a sudden fear, and – paradoxically – with an urgent desire to survive, he started to sink. And as the waves swallowed him he cried out, 'Lord, save me!'

Jesus immediately reached out to him. His hands were around him and beneath him, lifting him up, saving him, embracing him, and whispering in his ear, 'You of little faith, why did you doubt?'

Now Jesus held him again, held him with his eyes, and kept on holding his feet: 'Peter, don't you know this? Unless I wash you, you have no share with me.'

Jesus wanted something for Peter. It was there in the name he had given him. But Peter could still not get hold of it. And all Jesus could do was go on loving him.

There was then a difficult silence in the room. It seemed as if everyone was holding their breath. But Peter still wasn't ready to let go. He was still so very far from understanding, let alone receiving. 'Then not just my feet, but also my hands and my head,' he retorted indignantly and triumphantly, as if to say, 'Give me a bath, or nothing at all!'

Jesus said to him, 'One who has bathed does not need to wash, except for the feet, but is entirely clean. And you are clean, though not all of you.' None of them knew why he said this, though afterwards they realized it was because one of them was about to betray him.

Outside, darkness was falling. Inside, everything was changing. It was almost as if the shadow of night was passing across them inside the light of the room.

After he had washed their feet – Peter's feet, Judas' feet, everyone's feet – Jesus put his robe back on and returned to the table. He said to them, 'Do you know what I have done to you? You call me Teacher and Lord – and you are right, for that is what I am. So if I, your Lord and Teacher, have washed your feet, you also ought to wash one another's feet. For I have set you an example, that you also should do as I have done to you. Very truly, I tell you, servants are not greater than their master, nor are messengers greater than the one who sent them. If you know these things, you are blessed if you do them. I give you a new commandment, that you love one another. Just as I have loved you, you also should love one another. By this everyone will know that you are my disciples, if you have love for one another.'

This is what he did. He showed them what love looked like.

For reflection

- What did you make of this chapter?
- What feelings did it evoke in you? What experiences did it remind you of?
- What questions does it raise for you?

Read John 13.1–15.

- What strikes you most about this passage?
- Why do you think Peter found it so hard to let Jesus wash his feet?
- Whose feet would you least like to wash, and who would you least like to wash yours?
- What do you think Jesus is doing in this story?
- What was its meaning then, and what might be its meaning for us today?

5

He broke bread and shared wine

While they were at supper Jesus did what he had done with his disciples hundreds of times: he took bread and gave thanks to God.

On the face of it, there was nothing different about this. He simply took the bread. He lifted it up. He said the prayers of thanksgiving. This is what you do with bread. You cherish it. You eat it every day, but you don't take it for granted.

Bread is precious. Its daily blessing is the labour of the year. First there is the seed: the precious seed that you harvested from last year's crop and stored through the winter till the crocuses push through the earth and tell you it is spring and time for sowing. The ground is tilled and carefully prepared; prayers are offered and songs sung, and then the dead seed sown. Then, through the rains of spring and the hot months of summer, you labour and fret, clearing weeds and scaring birds till the grains are ripe for harvest. And the flour that you grind at the mill, or in a pestle in the kitchen, is bursting with the efforts of your labour and the memories of the harvest; and sprung by the miracle of yeast, and set aside for resurrection, or just mixed with water into the sticky paste that can also miraculously be bread, it is kneaded and pummelled into loaves. Above a lattice of flaming wood, also lovingly constructed, and deep in the womb of the oven, the marvel of daily bread is completed. Its warm fragrance rising through the house in the morning is the breath of life itself. Its texture torn open, burnt crust and soft white flesh, and its taste rolling round your mouth, is the quality and taste of home and of the satisfaction of belonging, of labour rewarded, of nature's many miracles, fruit of the earth and work of human hands. Yes, they had eaten with him many times, and he had blessed bread with them many times. But this time felt different. There was an eerie, interior silence about him that night. It had started when he had washed their feet, and now it continued around the supper table as they kept Passover together.

Earlier in the day he had given Peter and John some very specific instructions. He had told them to go and prepare the Passover meal. 'Where?' they had replied. 'And how?' And he had told them to go into the city where a man carrying a stone jar of water would meet them. They were to follow this man and he would lead them to a house where they should say to the owner, 'Where is the guest room, where our Master may eat the Passover with his friends?' And this man would show them a large room, already furnished, and this was where the preparations were to be made. So they went and found everything as Jesus had said, but they didn't understand how he had been able to make these arrangements, or why they needed to be quite so secretive. Though all his strange talk of suffering, and the way he had antagonized the authorities, did mean that they all felt marked out in some way; and in their different ways all of them were thinking, did it have to be like this? But they still got everything ready. A table set. A Passover lamb. Bread and wine.

The Passover; it was the meal that defined and sustained them, not just remembering what had happened that night in Egypt so long ago – the angel of death passing over the homes of the Hebrew slaves and striking the firstborn of Egypt; the beginning of an exodus through the wilderness to a promised land flowing with honey and milk; Pharaoh's horses and chariots swallowed by the sea while they passed through the waters – but in the economy of a God for whom a thousand years is but a watch in the night, this remembering of what God had done for them in the past brought the same God's salvation and saving love into the present. It was as if the Passover of Moses and *their* Passover on *this* night was one and the same. The past was not a thing of the past. It was the eternal now of the eternal God, breaking into their present. God would save them and liberate them as he had saved and liberated Moses. This is what they believed, and this was the meaning of the Passover for them: a sacred and holy meal in which God delivered them again.

Oh, how they needed this deliverance. How they longed for it. How they felt enslaved and diminished by the Roman occupation and by what seemed to be the gutless compromises of those who led them. And though they liked to convince themselves that their cause was noble and their agenda righteous (oh, yes, how they loved to be seen as righteous), deeper still, so many other enslavements also swilled around inside their muddled hearts: that all too obvious and common desire for power, riches and rank that had already raised its ugly head that week; and baser desires for the easy gratifications of lust and violence. It was all there; all boiling inside them as they prayed for deliverance. Even the bitter treachery of wanting to destroy, to annihilate and to possess; and that very human condition: to desire that which will kill you. It raged in them. All the things they longed for, and at the same time longed to be released from.

And the hopes they had in Jesus? None of them seemed sure any more. None of them knew what he was doing. They could see the things he did, but it no longer made any sense. And Jesus himself looked round at their confused faces, and it was as if he could see right inside their despair and their hope to be free from despairing.

He held the bread aloft, the bread that was fruit of the earth, that was work of human hands, that was the very stuff of life, and he gave thanks to God for all God's provision and bounty, for all God's goodness and power. This was the God they loved, the God they saw in Jesus, but the God they still couldn't understand. This was the God who would bring destruction to the earth – but not as the fanatics and fundamentalists had it, the earth itself being destroyed, or the people upon it who didn't quite fit, or who believed different things, or who belonged to another tribe, or whose skin was pale – but the God who would destroy war itself, who would shatter the bow and snap the spear and burn the chariots of fire; the God who would judge between nations, and arbitrate for many people, and beat swords into ploughshares, and spears into pruning hooks, so that nations will no longer lift up swords against each other and they would stop investing in war.

Then he broke the bread. He tore the loaf in two, and his arms were stretched wide as he held out the bread to them. It looked as if he was going to embrace them as well as feed them. At the same time he looked suddenly very vulnerable, like he was being stretched out on a rack. 'Take, eat,' he said. 'This is my body which is given for you.'

Then he took the cup of wine. Again he held it aloft and gave thanks to God. He said that Israel was a vine, and that God was a vinedresser, and that God would prune and perfect, that things that were cut down grew again, and that seeds buried in dry ground blossomed. He then passed the cup around; and as he did this he said, 'Drink this, all of you; this is my blood of the new covenant, which is shed for you and for many for the forgiveness of sins. Do this, as often as you drink it, in remembrance of me.'

And they remembered. Not just what Moses had done and what God had done in Moses, but they remembered what Jesus had said and done. They remembered how he had said that he was a vine like Israel, and they branches, and that cut off from him they could do nothing. They remembered how he had said that he was bread, bread of life; that he was food and drink; that his flesh eaten and his blood drunk, was life; that Moses on that journey to deliverance had been given manna from heaven, but he and all those who had eaten that bread were dead, but that those who ate the bread that was his body would live for ever, that he was the living bread come down from heaven.

They remembered this; and at the same time they recoiled from it, for he was also speaking of a new covenant that was somehow made by his blood shed and his body broken, and that in some curious way that they could not comprehend he was offering it to them now, in this broken bread and this cup shared. Somehow their eating and drinking, the things they did with him this night, were making something new, were preparing for something tumultuous that was somehow tied up with all that other talk of suffering and death.

Who was he? What was he about to do? There was joy in his presence around that table. But there was also fear.

Before the meal Jesus had said quite openly that one of them would betray him and that all of them would desert him. They had looked at him incredulously. 'Is it I?' they had said, one after the other, each one asserting their innocence. But they had looked at each other accusingly, only too pleased to believe the worst about their neighbour.

Peter had promised that whatever anyone else did he could be relied on, that he would never betray or desert him. As usual, he was carried away by his own rhetoric. It wasn't only Jesus who knew that, like so many orators, he was only really trying to persuade himself. He wanted to be brave and true. But he wasn't. Therefore his words had to be brave and true instead.

One of them – Judas Iscariot – slipped out into the night. Jesus had washed his feet too. Jesus had shared bread with him. But Judas' mind was made up, his path mapped out. He had lost all confidence in what Jesus was doing. He believed that Jesus, too, had been overtaken by his own rhetoric.

Judas no longer believed that Jesus was the Messiah. He had believed this. But not any more. After all, messiahs didn't walk second miles or turn other cheeks, or give bandits two cloaks when they asked for one. Messiahs didn't say that the kingdom belonged to children. They didn't produce ridiculous amounts of wine for already half-drunk wedding guests, or let expensive ointment be wasted. They didn't let dubious women wash their feet with their hair, and they didn't wash other people's feet in return. They didn't demean themselves. They didn't get in the way of justice, by letting adulterers walk free; and they didn't shame those who were simply carrying out what the law so clearly required. And they certainly didn't speak of themselves as if they were God, rather than just the one God sent. To speak of his own body as if it was bread from heaven: this was blasphemy, and Judas couldn't understand why he had not seen it clearly before. In fact, the more he thought about it, the more he burned with righteous anger, knowing that his actions, and the things he was now going to do, would save his people from the threat that Jesus posed. All this talk of love, and of a new commandment and a new coven-ant, achieved nothing other than the disintegration of all that the old covenant held together. And even if he had got it wrong, even if Jesus was the Messiah, even if all this meekness was a cover, and if he was about to do what really needed to be done and deal with apostasy, the anath-ema of foreign occupation, and the invidious infection of disbelief and evil – and actually this was still something Judas secretly hoped for – then it was only right to bring things to a head, to allow things to be *unconcealed*. So he had brokered a deal with the chief priests and the religious authorities. For a modest fee, he would now show them where to find Jesus.

The other disciples watched him go. They didn't really know why he was going, though one or two suspected something. Jesus also watched him. He just looked at him steadily and loved him.

Silence fell upon the room. One or two of the candles guttered and went out. The dying of the light, like the death of a man, is rarely a dramatic thing. It just stops. Those lights that were left cast looming shadows across the table, so that some of them sat in darkness, and where there was light it flickered upon their faces as if it was about to die as well. Which it was. All over the city, lights were going out. The day was ending. And though they hoped for a new covenant, like the one God had made with Moses, they just couldn't see it. And all this talk of suffering and death, of bodies broken and blood shed, it just frightened them, and they felt further away from God than ever; and with Jesus slipping before their eyes into the shadows of what seemed to be an all-consuming night, their faith in him was stretched to breaking point. How ironic! Not just the bread broken. Not just him broken, but their faith in him. How could he deliver Israel? How could he deliver them? How could he even save himself? Forces even darker than the dark night seemed to be lining up against him, moving into position, preparing for a kill. How could he stop them? He no longer seemed to them to be a prophet, or even a visionary, still less a Messiah. There was strength in him, in his silence, in that inexhaustible goodness and compassion that still held them to him around that table – but could love ever be enough? They doubted it. He was a dreamer, a child, a table-turner and a foot-washer, a weaver of beautiful dreams, a storyteller and a lover, a wonderful fountain of goodness and love, but not a liberator or a God. And these dark forces would crush him.

The bread was eaten. The wine was drunk. The meal was finished. Jesus led them out into the night. They didn't know where they were going.

'Do this to remember me,' he had said. They didn't know what this meant. But they would remember. For the things he did that night would unlock the meaning of what he did next.

For reflection

- What did you make of this chapter?
- What feelings did it evoke in you? What experiences did it remind you of?
- What questions does it raise for you?

Read Matthew 26.17–30.

- What strikes you most about this passage?
- What do you think the disciples made of Jesus' words and actions at the Last Supper?
- How does what happens at the Last Supper help us to understand his cross and resurrection?
- What do you think Jesus is doing in this story?
- What was its meaning then, and what might be its meaning for us today?

6

*He prayed that there might
be another way*

Life outside or beyond this life is unimaginable. That is why we hold on to life. That is why the smallest death, even the roadkill swept into the gutter, is a reminder of our own. We see the spilt blood, the unravelled viscera, the private parts, the tubes and compartments inside us that go about their business pumping life and maintaining health, and we privately offer thanks that this death is not ours. Not yet.

There were no corpses on the road that night. Not yet.

Jesus led them out of the house and through the winding roads of Jerusalem to a garden at the edge of the city called Gethsemane.

No one spoke. Even the moon was shrouded by dark cloud and it was hard to see the path ahead. Somewhere in the distance an owl hooted.

One of them stumbled and nearly fell. Everyone laughed. For a moment the tension eased. The fire under the kettle went out. The shrill, insistent whistling stopped. Jesus, too, turned round and smiled. These men, in whom he had invested so much, stared back at him grinning stupidly. He had laboured with them so long, but they comprehended so little. Only love could save them now.

The fire re-ignites. The water boils. The whistling resumes. People put their fingers in their ears. They pretend that this is how it is meant to be. Life goes on. Unchanged. Unconcealed.

When they got to Gethsemane, Jesus took Peter, James and John to one side. He had done this before. They were the three that he particularly trusted. He said that he was going to pray, and asked them to watch and pray with him. He seemed anxious, even agitated. It was as if some weight was bearing down on him, and that he was being given something to carry that was hard and heavy.

He left them in the corner of the garden by a large spiny hawthorn bush and walked a few paces into the centre, about a stone's throw away from them. The heavy blossom of Spanish broom and acacia hung in the night air: the long-stemmed flowers of the broom and the round fleecy spheres of the acacia formed a yellow canopy that he walked under into a clearing in the centre of the garden. Wild gladiola, yellow daisies and purple thistle peppered the grass. Like a sailor lost at sea, he looked up into the gathering blackness of the night sky, searching out the position of the moon or the familiarity of a star, scanning the horizon for something that could give him a bearing. But there was nothing. His grip on life was loosening. The once steady compass of his faithfulness was spinning wildly inside him. Fear seized him, and he fell to his knees on the dry, unforgiving earth. The blood of Abel cried out for vengeance; and he too cried out, saying to God, if it is possible take this cup away from me.

This was the darkest moment: his pleading with God that there might be another way. He knelt down on the cold ground and wept like a child; and he cried out as a child might cry to his mother, asking for something that it first believes can be given, and then slowly realizes must be withheld, not because there is no love, but because this is what love requires. The words that he had said about walking second miles and turning other cheeks and giving enemies a drink, they were now focused into these moments of foreboding, for now he had to prepare himself (if preparation is possible) to do what he had said.

He turned to look for the support of his friends, to lean upon their good wishes and their prayers, but they were fast asleep. The turmoil of the day and the gentle irrigation of the wine had overtaken them. They hid from their fears in the comfort of sleep, and were able to give him no comfort.

Jesus stared at them. For a brief moment, the frustration and the agony inside him boiled into fleeting anger. He shook them awake and reprimanded them. 'Could you not even stay awake one hour?' They rubbed their eyes and offered excuses. They made a few more promises they would never keep. With sobering resignation, he remembered why he was here: to confront these failures and their dreadful consequences. Why be surprised? The spirit is willing, but the flesh is weak. So he urged them, 'Try and stay awake. Please pray with me.'

The temperature was dropping. Days in Jerusalem are fearfully hot, but the nights are stone cold. A cool evening breeze, and the late hour, and the approaching deadness of the night brought an added chill. Jesus returned to where he had been kneeling and looked again into the sky. For a few moments the clouds parted and the full face of the full moon beamed upon him, filling the night with soft, milky light. Behind the moon the astonishing, dazzling panoply of space. This frightening, fragile world is very beautiful. Its wonders unending. Its joys supreme. He stood there as the glow from long-dead stars washed over him, reflecting in the liquid white of his brooding eyes.

It was impossible to imagine death. Dying, yes, and its concomitant agonies, but the 'not-being' of death itself, and the emptiness of centuries that would not hold the possibility of life, this could not be imagined, though the starlight that beamed upon him was the last bright flash of that star's death.

He turned again, and looked towards Peter and the others. They had already collapsed back into sleep. Their breath was as heavy as his heart.

He was alone. Alone with the night and all its challenges; and waiting alone for all that lay beyond him in the morning.

He cried out again: 'If it is possible, let this cup pass from me. If it is possible, take this away.' But now he was shivering with fear as well as cold.

Hadn't he already tasted it? Wasn't that what he was saying earlier with the bread and the wine?

Wasn't that why he had rebuked James and John when they had asked for places at his left and right, and said that they could drink his cup? Because he knew what was in it, knew its purpose and its taste?

His flesh could be bread, and like bread must be broken. His blood could be wine, and like wine must be poured out: this cup of suffering, this cup of faithfulness that only he could drink, it was being lifted to his lips. He could smell its thick odour; he could anticipate its taste.

It had always been waiting for him. From the moment he had gone down into the waters, and John had said, 'Look, here is the Lamb of God', this day had been coming. He didn't know quite how it would work out, or how it would end, but this much was clear: he had to take this cup and drain it to the dregs.

With this bitter conclusion, his whole body convulsed and he prayed all the more fervently, no longer asking for the cup to be removed, but for the strength to drink it. Like the servant Isaiah had spoken of, he now prayed that he might be the faithful one who waits and suffers, the one who even in anguish might see light, and even wounded might make others whole. He didn't know how. He only knew what he had to do; and as he prayed the sweat fell from his body like great drops of blood. This was his final prayer: 'Your will be done, not mine.'

When he returned to the disciples, they were sound asleep. His abandonment was almost complete. 'Are you still sleeping? Are you still taking your rest?' he said to them.

They stirred, looking at him blankly. They didn't know what to say and they didn't know what to do. But knowing what was nearly upon him, hearing other noises in the garden and the sound of urgent footsteps on the path, he said to them, 'See, the hour is at hand, and the Son of Man is betrayed into the hands of sinners. Get up, let us be going. See, my betrayer is at hand.'

And while he was still speaking, Judas arrived; and with him a large crowd with swords and clubs, from the chief priests and the elders of the people. All of a sudden they were around him, cutting him off from his friends. He felt their hot breath on his face.

Now the betrayer had given them a sign, saying, 'The one I will kiss is the man; arrest him.' So he came up to Jesus and bowed before him, but he wouldn't look him in the eye. Not yet. 'Greetings, Rabbi!' he said, and kissed him. Jesus froze for a moment as he received that kiss. For this is not how kisses are meant to be. That which denotes friendship and affection, that which is reserved for intimacy and passion, that which is the sign of love and love's intent, was now a cheap and nasty thing, a sign of love's betrayal. The traitor's lips only brushed his cheek, barely touched his flesh, but their resolve was slick and plain, their wetness still enough to stain. This was the man who had walked with him, who had sat at his feet and learned from him. This was the man he had trusted, the man whose feet he had washed and who shared his bread. Jesus looked at him with an aching sadness, for he still loved him, even though this was now the beginning of the heavy price of love, all the things he was about to carry. He knew it was for such as these – for moments like this and for people like Judas – that he had come: those who got it wrong; those who rejected and betrayed; those who received bread but were never filled; those who chose to be hungry because they were still hell-bent on commanding others; those who could never let go, and who could never let anyone else in; those who because they knew how to control others had forgotten how to love them. In fact, they couldn't love anyone, especially not themselves. So Judas kissed him, and Jesus said to him, 'Friend, do what you are here to do.'

Then they were upon him. They knew which one to take. They seized him. They laid their strong hands on him. They dug their nails into his flesh. They arrested him. But Peter was indignant; the sap of his rage was rising. He moved from slumber to vengeance in a single bound. He rushed forward, and drawing his sword struck out at the slave of the high priest and cut off his ear. It was a horrid, grubby little moment of stupid and savage violence. In fact, it was like every act of violence – unnecessary, senseless and shocking. It happened because people are stupid, and as much because they cannot love themselves as because of their failure to love others, for if you despise yourself enough you will quickly accrue the courage for violence. Without knowing it you will have already deemed yourself eligible for reprisal. You will value no one. You will just want to stamp and rage and have things your way, though, sadly, you will not even know what your way is, except the downward spiral of violence and revenge, of hatred and more hatred and death. It was into this furious whirlwind of violence that Peter so easily stepped. And it was to hang at the heart of the whirlwind and extinguish its powers with love by drawing it all to himself, that Jesus came that night to do what he had to do, to drink the cup of suffering and to do the Father's will. His wrath would be turned on wrath itself. His vengeance would be on the cruelty and deceit of death. His battle would be with sin and all its bloody, violent horror. And he would do it with patient suffering and with exhausting and inexhaustible love.

Those in the crowd reached for their weapons. For a moment it seemed there would be a blood bath. But Jesus shook himself free and took command. He stepped a pace forward, also furious, but with a righteous indignation that would not strike out: the very power of love. 'Put your sword back into its place,' he said to Peter angrily, bravely, 'for all who take the sword will perish by the sword.'

Then speaking to those who were holding him he appealed to them: 'Have you come out with swords and clubs to arrest me as though I were a bandit? Day after day I was with you in the Temple teaching, and you did not arrest me. But let the scriptures be fulfilled.' And as he said this the disciples turned and fled. They no longer wanted any part in this fulfilment. And they were terrified.

Those who were around him, held him again, only tighter, and with a fearfulness and dread. What was this fulfilment he spoke of? He was to them, on the one hand, just another false prophet, an empty vessel to be crushed. But also something else. Like the line of a melody you cannot quite remember, but whose beauty haunts you; they knew and they didn't know who he was, and they couldn't forget him, nor put him away easily, even though he gave them no resistance.

All the disciples were gone. The night was cold and dark.

Peter followed at a distance. Most people do. When questioned later, he claimed he didn't even know Jesus. He wasn't really lying. Most people don't know him.

A certain young man, I think his name might have been Mark, still followed. They caught him, but he slipped from their grasp leaving them holding nothing but the linen cloth he had been wearing. He ran off naked into the night.

Jesus too was now falling and blending into the night, into the arms of darkness. He was alone with his destiny. There was one more thing he had to do.

'Who is this that comes from Edom,
from Bozrah in garments stained crimson?
Who is this so splendidly robed,
    marching in his great might?'

'It is I, announcing vindication,
    mighty to save.'

'Why are your robes red,
    and your garments like theirs who tread the wine press?'

'I have trodden the wine press alone,
    and from the peoples no one was with me;
I trod them in my anger
    and trampled them in my wrath;
their juice spattered on my garments
    and stained all my robes.
For the day of vengeance was in my heart,
    and the year for my redeeming work had come.
I looked, but there was no helper;
    I stared, but there was no one to sustain me.'

Isaiah 63.1–5

For reflection

- What did you make of this chapter?
- What feelings did it evoke in you? What experiences did it remind you of?
- What questions does it raise for you?

Read Matthew 26.36–56.

- What strikes you most about this passage?
- Have you ever had the experience of knowing there is something you must do, but hoping there might be another way?
- And if you feel able to, share experiences when you have let someone down, or even betrayed someone you loved, or responded with violence and anger; or been let down or betrayed or hurt.
- What do you think Jesus is doing in this story?
- What was its meaning then, and what might be its meaning for us today?

A prayer

Dear God,
You let your walking do your talking
And your word is always made flesh.
Show me what to do by looking at the things you did
And doing them myself.
Let this be how people know I'm your disciple.
Amen.

Did you know that SPCK is a registered charity?

As well as publishing great books by leading Christian authors, we also . . .

. . . make assemblies meaningful and fun for over a million children by running www.assemblies.org.uk, a popular website that provides free assembly scripts for teachers. For many children, school assembly is the only contact they have with Christian faith and culture, and the only time in their week for spiritual reflection.

. . . help prisoners to become confident readers with our easy-to-read stories. Poor literacy is a huge barrier to rehabilitation. Prisoners identify with the believable heroes of our gritty fiction. At the same time, questions at the end of each chapter help them to examine their choices from a moral perspective and to build their reading confidence.

. . . support student ministers overseas in their training through partnerships in the Global South.

Please support these great schemes: visit www.spck.org.uk/support-us to find out more.